Growing Readers
New Hanover County Public Library
DISCARDED
from
New Hanover County Public Library
Purchased with
New Hanover County Partnership for Children
and Smart Start Funds

Let's Read About Our Bodies

Nose

by Cynthia Klingel* and Robert B. Noyed
photographs by Gregg Andersen

* Amoroso is preferred name

Reading consultant: Cecilia Minden-Cupp, Ph.D.,
Adjunct Professor, College of Continuing and Professional Studies, University of Virginia

WeeklyReader.
EARLY LEARNING LIBRARY

For a free color catalog describing Weekly Reader® Early Learning Library's list of high-quality books, call 1-800-542-2595 or fax your request to (414) 332-3567.

Library of Congress Cataloging-in-Publication Data

Klingel, Cynthia.
Nose / by Cynthia Klingel and Robert B. Noyed.
p. cm. – (Let's read about our bodies)
Includes bibliographical references and index.
Summary: An introduction to the nose, what it is used for, and how to take care of it.
ISBN 0-8368-3068-7 (lib. bdg.)
ISBN 0-8368-3157-8 (softcover)
1. Nose–Juvenile literature. 2. Smell–Juvenile literature. [1. Nose. 2. Smell. 3. Senses and sensation.] I. Noyed, Robert B. II. Title.
QP458.K553 2002
611'.21–dc21 2001055054

This edition first published in 2002 by
Weekly Reader® Early Learning Library
330 West Olive Street, Suite 100
Milwaukee, WI 53212 USA

An Editorial Directions book
Editors: E. Russell Primm and Emily Dolbear
Art direction, design, and page production: The Design Lab
Photographer: Gregg Andersen
Weekly Reader® Early Learning Library art direction: Tammy Gruenewald
Weekly Reader® Early Learning Library production: Susan Ashley

Printed in the United States of America

1 2 3 4 5 6 7 8 9 06 05 04 03 02

Note to Educators and Parents

As a Reading Specialist I know that books for young children should engage their interest, impart useful information, and motivate them to want to learn more.

Let's Read About Our Bodies is a new series of books designed to help children understand the value of good health and taking care of their bodies.

A young child's active mind is engaged by the carefully chosen subjects. The imaginative text works to build young vocabularies. The short, repetitive sentences help children stay focused as they develop their own relationship with reading. The bright, colorful photographs of children enjoying good health habits complement the text with their simplicity and both entertain and encourage young children to want to learn – and read – more.

These books are designed to be used by adults as "read-to" books to share with children to encourage early literacy in the home, school, and library. They are also suitable for more advanced young readers to enjoy on their own.

– Cecilia Minden-Cupp, Ph.D.,
Adjunct Professor, College of Continuing and Professional Studies, University of Virginia

This is my nose.
I like to wiggle
my nose.

I use my nose to smell lots of things.

Some things smell yummy.

Some things smell stinky!

I use my nose to breathe.

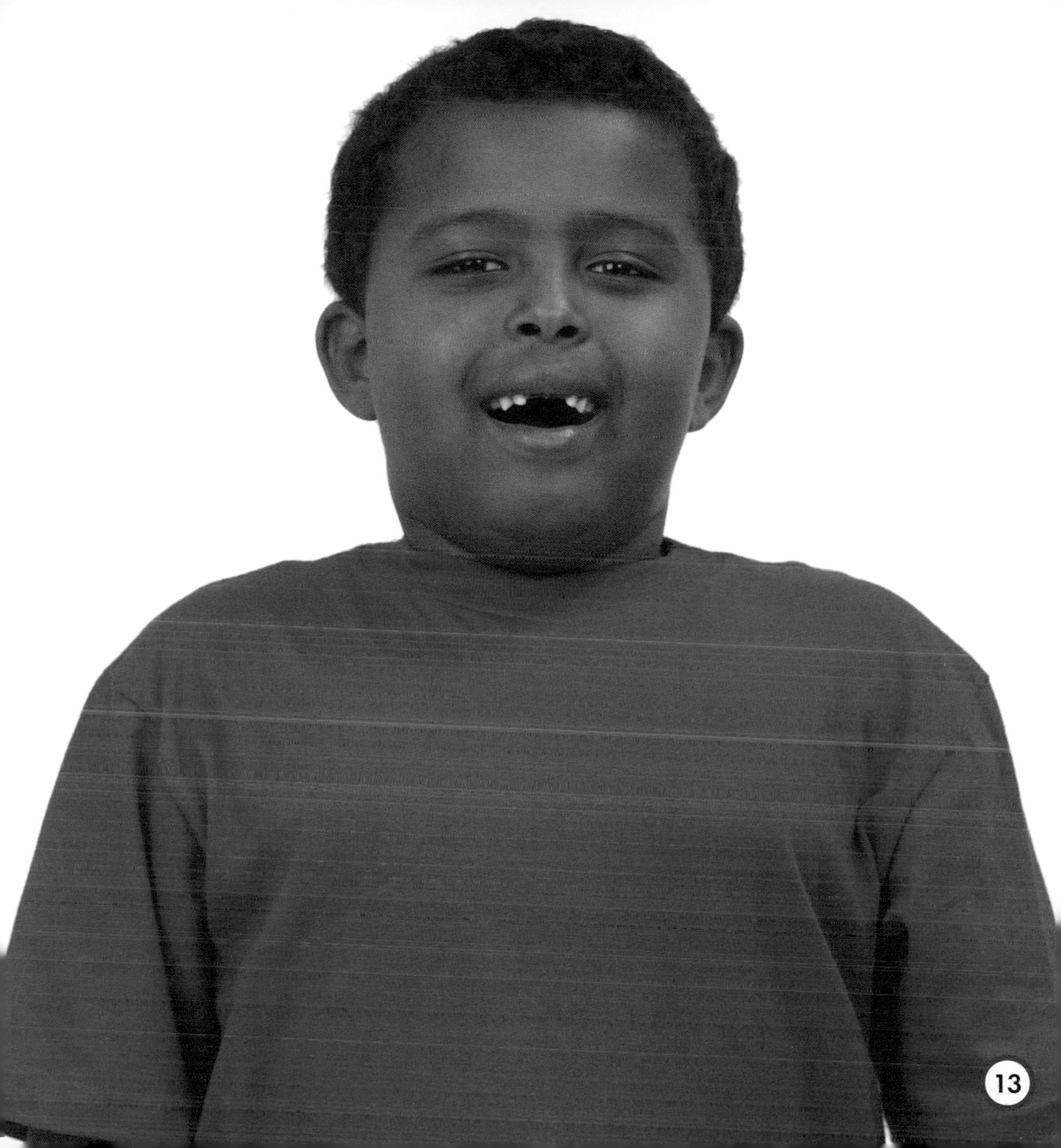

Some things make me sneeze. Pepper, flour, and dust make me sneeze.

Sometimes I get a stuffy nose.

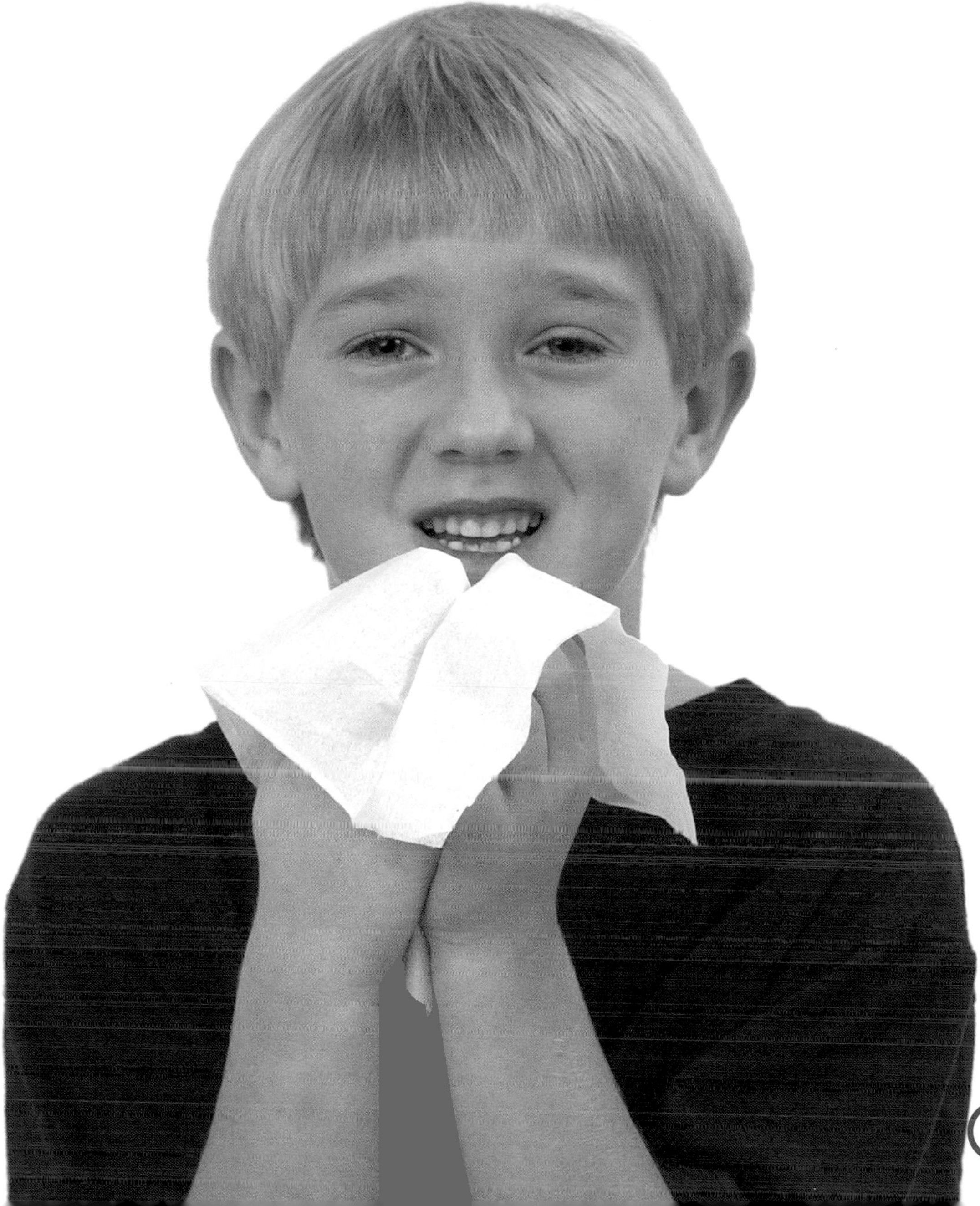

Sometimes I have a runny nose. Then I need to wipe my nose.

I am careful to take care of my nose.

Glossary

breathe—to take air into the lungs and then let it out

sneeze—air forced from the nose and mouth in a sudden way

stuffy—closed up

yummy—good tasting

For More Information

Fiction Books

Brown, Marc Tolon. *Arthur's Nose*. Boston: Little Brown & Co., 1986.

Caple, Kathy. *The Biggest Nose*. Boston: Houghton Mifflin Co., 1988.

Faulkner, Keith. *The Long-Nosed Pig*. New York: Dial Books for Young Readers, 1998.

Nonfiction Books

Fowler, Allan. *Knowing about Noses*. New York: HarperCollins Juvenile Books, 1991.

Moses, Brian. *Munching, Crunching, Sniffling, and Snooping*. New York: DK Publishing, 1999.

Web Sites

What's That Smell? The Nose Knows

kidshealth.org/kid/body/nose_SW.html

For information about the different parts of the nose

Index

About the Authors

Cynthia Klingel has worked as a high school English teacher and an elementary school teacher. She is currently the curriculum director for a Minnesota school district. Cynthia Klingel lives with her family in Mankato, Minnesota.

Robert B. Noyed started his career as a newspaper reporter. Since then, he has worked in school communications and public relations at the state and national level. Robert B. Noyed lives with his family in Brooklyn Center, Minnesota.